# Montessori Inspired Activities for Pre-Schoolers

Jo Ebisujima

Published by Little Ebi Publishing



ISBN-13: 978-0-9927079-0-3

Your free bonus
3 part cards and handy printables
download at
http://bit.ly/MontessoriInspiredFreebies

# Why You Should Read This Book

If you have a pre-schooler, you obviously want to help them with their development. There are expensive toys and equipment out there with all the 'bells and whistles', but you could be helping your child without having to pay for them.

Many activities can be set up at home, with items that you already have or are inexpensive to buy. This also cuts down on the ever increasing clutter of plastic and new toys that the child loses interest in, within a matter of days or sometimes even hours.

I fell in love with the Montessori philosophy when my son was a baby but on a whole, Montessori equipment is very expensive, more so if you only have one child. This book is a collection of activities that we did at home that didn't require buying or making any specialized equipment, making it easy for you to help your little one develop their skills.

# Dedication

I would like to thank all the people who have supported and helped me over the years since we embarked on our Montessori journey. A special thank you to Linda Cameron and Meg Anderson McElwee for all their help in the early years, without them we wouldn't have made it this far!

Also to all the bloggers who share their amazing ideas – when we started our journey they were few and far between – and the dedicated moms who put the information they find out there for us all to share.

Thanks to my best friend Di, who has always supported my ideas, however crackpot-like they might be.

Not forgetting, of course my fantastic husband and son who have grown into this Montessori inspired life of ours. Without them, this journey would never have even started.

# CONTENTS

*"The environment must be rich in motives which lend interest to activity and invite the child to conduct his own experiences."*

~Maria Montessori

# Introduction

I dived into the world of blogging back in 2007, sharing the activities and crafty things I was doing with my son and writing about our life in Japan.

When my son (known as Ebi-kun in online world) was a baby I took an online Montessori course. Sadly we didn't have a Montessori school nearby so I set about teaching him from home. We couldn't afford to set up a room in the same way that you set up a school, and so I ended up making many things for him to use. As we went along our journey, I blogged about what we were doing.

All the activities in the book have been tried and tested and blogged about. I've collected them all together and added the link for downloads in one place to make life easier for busy parents like yourself. Use it as you please: you may want to set up a shelf as part of a homeschool space or you might want to just pick out an activity at random when you need your little people to be occupied.

All the activities have some kind of educational reasoning behind them, be it awareness of the senses, pincer muscle strengthening or basic kitchen science. Most, but not all, are taken from the Montessori curriculum.

The activities are written as the original blog posts, in some cases extra information has been given to make it clearer so they are the same format. The activities are not presented in the order that we did them, instead they have been grouped for easy reference for you.

Although these activities were used with my son between the ages of 18 months and 4 years old, many of them can be repeated as the child gets older and their depth and understanding of the world around them grows. Almost all activities can be done repeatedly and if you have your room set up with a few activities on the shelf, you will see that you child will be drawn to one or two as they progress through a learning cycle.

Some activities include free printables which you can access by signing up at http://bit.ly/MontessoriInspiredFreebies.

None of the activities need specialized Montessori equipment, many you will be able to put together today with the items you have around the home. If you don't have the exact equipment at hand, use your imagination and use what you do have.

There are not many activities that are focused on reading and writing, because we used mostly Montessori equipment for that and I wanted the focus of this book to be on non-specialized equipment. In addition we didn't follow the usual steps when it came to reading. Ebi-kun knew his letters at two, was reading at three and was on his first chapter book at four. It is easy to fall into the comparison trap with kids and I wanted to avoid that.

Generally speaking, in a Montessori classroom the children start working with language materials in the 3-6 class, I will include more of these type of activities in the next book.

# A Word Of Caution

Always supervise children doing experiments at home and take care with small objects used for spooning, scooping, etc. as they can pose as a choking threat.

# A Note About Using Glass

As a Montessori family, we have always used glass and ceramic plates, dishes and cups. Part of Maria Montessori's theory is that if a child is taught to use things properly from the start they will respect the things around them. From a very early age, we told Ebi-kun that if he broke something, like a plate, that he shouldn't touch it but should come and tell us. We have never had an issue with him cutting himself and in 8 years we have only ever had one accident with a broken plate (he sobbed for about half an hour and no, he wasn't scolded for breaking it, he was genuinely upset).

By giving children the responsibility to be careful with their possessions from an early age it will help them grow up to be more responsible and careful.

If you want to start using 'real' cups, plates and glasses but don't want to get out the best family china, try looking in thrift stores or charity shops. Many Asian countries use small dishes at meal times and are perfect sizes for little hands. Ikea also do some cute stoneware sets suitable for kids.

If you're not comfortable with using breakable items and will lose sleep over it, then don't do it. I am just explaining why I give my son a glass or ceramic jugs to work with,but the decision at the end of the day is yours to make.

# About Montessori

Montessori is an educational philosophy developed by the Italian, DR Maria Montessori. It is based on her years of research in special education. Montessori education has a strong emphasis on independence and encourages curiosity and spontaneous activity by the child.

The classroom and home is a prepared environment where equipment is designed for children not adults, beauty and cleanliness are emphasized and the materials are limited to what will support the child's development. One other unique idea Montessori had was mixed aged classes. Younger children learn from their peers and older children become the teachers, developing cooperation and empathy within the class. This can be used with siblings too, the older becomes the teacher.

There is so much to say about the Montessori philosophy and not enough space for me to do it here. Instead, I encourage you to read Maria Montessori's own books, starting with The Absorbent Mind.

# Work cycles

In a traditional Montessori classroom, the activities are laid out on the shelves and the children work with whatever calls to them. If you watch your child you will notice that they will often get engrossed in a specific kind of work for a number or days, sometime weeks. It might be that they can't get enough of numbers and counting or maybe they are going through a sensory period and they are only really interested in sensory activities.

Often at home, we don't have the space to set up a whole classroom full of activities so it is important to observe your child and notice what it is they are being drawn to, then you can make sure you are providing the right type of activities for their needs.

None of the activities in this book have ages attached to them, as it is difficult to know when each child is ready for each activity. For many of the activities the child will come back to it repeatedly, getting more out of it each time they do it. It is 5 years since we first did the volcano experiment and my son still loves it and his knowledge deepens each time he does it. I recommend reading through the activities and try to imagine if it is something your child can do. The best way is to set it up and see what happens.

In a Montessori environment, children are shown the whole process of an activity, from taking it off the shelf to tidying and putting it all away before starting on the next thing. This is a really important part of the learning process and helps children learn how to fully complete a project rather than leaving it midway. Toddlers will often need help or prompting to put everything away after finishing an activity, I found that just being firm and reminding my son that we have to put everything away before choosing something else was usually enough to get the job done. Now, he does it without thinking.

One more note: Sometimes you will present a new activity and it will be a total flop, the child won't be interested and you are left wondering why you bother. Don't give up, maybe the activity was not the right one at the right time, try to introduce it again a few weeks later or just leave it on the shelf and see if your child takes an interest when left to their own devices.

# How To Present A Lesson

This method is used across the board for introducing ideas to children in a Montessori environment and it is exceptionally useful for introducing new vocabulary. It is an easy idea to learn but you should practice without a child before getting stuck in. There is nothing complicated, keeping it simple is the best way forward.

**Stage 1**
Start by setting out three objects or cards on a mat or at the table, in front of your child. As remembering things at the start and end of a list is easier, put the easiest object to recall in the middle. For this example we will use 3 artists. The naming period is just that, name the object/card.

Point to the first card and say "A Van Gogh"

Repeat several times then ask "Can you say Van Gogh?"

The child may or may not repeat the word, don't worry about it, just continue.

Now point to the second card and say "A Monet" repeat as you did with the first card and then go through with card three.

Ask the child to point to each card in turn "Can you point to the Klimt card?", etc.

**Stage 2**
Shuffle the cards and lay them out again. Use the following style questions to get the child to show they recognize the cards, again, don't worry if they don't talk. This period will take longer, shuffle the cards or objects a number of times and think of variations to keep the lesson interesting. Maybe

moving around the room, placing the cards in a different area of the room for the child to fetch – make it fun! The kinesthetic movement associated with this part of the lesson helps with the child's memory and recall of the objects/cards.

"Show me the Klimt card please"

"Point to the Van Gogh card"

"Pass me the Monet card please"

"Put the Van Gogh in the basket"

"Put the Klimt on the shelf"

**Stage 3**
IMPORTANT: you should not start this stage unless you are confident that the child can succeed. If the child is not yet ready, continue with stage 2. Ifthe child can't recall the names of the object or cards then do a quick recap and then finish the lesson, end it on a high note so that the child doesn't feel like they have failed.

This is like the testing stage of the lesson and it should be the first time you ask the child to recall the names of the objects.

Put the cards or objects in front of the child and ask

"What is this?"

Repeat with the other objects, just to be sure, shuffle and repeat.

# Practical Life

Practical Life is one of the main areas of study in the Montessori environment. The activities always have a practical side to them, learning to fold, to look after plants or learning to pour without making a mess. Many of the activities also have a secondary reason behind them, often they will be helping the child learn about length or depth or to strengthen their pincer muscles that are used for writing. What might appear to be a boring activity to an adult is often challenging and fascinating to a child who is still learning about their world and how their body works.

**From the blog...**
www.jojoebi-designs.com

We have some practical life activities set up on the shelf but Ebi-kun doesn't bother with them much, the exception being the pouring and spooning activities. That said, he does get his fair share of practical life experiences by helping me around the house, he sorts the socks when I am hanging out the laundry and puts away most of his own clothes (he can't quite manage getting his T-shirts in the drawer yet), he also puts away some of my laundry in the drawers he can reach. He helps with the dusting and cleaning and has just started to lay the table ready for lunch.

In the morning he helps unload the dishwasher putting the dishes away and sorting the cutlery. He also folds all the napkins and puts them away, yet he won't touch the folding exercise on the shelf. Whenever I am in the kitchen he wants to help, so yesterday I had him grating the peel off some yuzu.

So, what I think I am try to say is that although at Montessori schools 'practical life' activities are important and sometimes the only way for a child to practice is by doing a shelf type activity, I think at home they should be off the shelf and put into context, folding napkins that are used everyday at the table and putting them in the drawer has more meaning that folding some towels and putting them in a basket on a shelf where they only get used as a folding activity.

Sorting cutlery and putting it away in the kitchen drawer is more interesting than doing it at a little table then putting it back on the shelf. As is preparing a snack, pouring milk rather than coloured water and spooning sweet beans into a dish for dinner rather than dry beans as a table activity.

There are many activities that children can help with around the home and toddlers love to help out, so give them some jobs to do.

## *Notes and observations*

# The Activities

*"The first essential for the child's development is concentration. The child who concentrates is immensely happy."*

~Maria Montessori

# Flower Arranging

Finally Ebi-kun has got the hang of putting the flowers the right way in the vase. I have to try to keep an eye on him though because he likes to get the vase to smell the flowers, which usually results in water everywhere - and then he cries because he has spilt the water. He is getting better though, he recently started to climb on the chair and just sniff from a distance.

**What you need:**

- A small vase
- A jug of water
- A cloth for spills
- A tray to work on

Pick a few flowers from the garden or buy a small posy. Give the child a tray with a small vase, a jug with water and a cloth in case of spills.

Ask the child to put the water in the vase. Then ask them to arrange the flowers. Some children many want to dissect the flowers instead of arranging them, that is OK, ask the child to put most in the vase and keep a couple to examine. It is a good idea to have a magnifying glass handy!

This is both a sensory activity and a practical life one. Use the child's arrangement to decorate the dining table at meal times.

# Spooning

Here is Ebi-kun with one of his spooning exercises. I picked up the wooden spoon, bowl and tray from the ¥100 shop (like the dollar store), the glass jar used to have cinnamon in it (from our wedding in Cambodia) the best thing is that it still smells of cinnamon and has scented the beans - lovely! The spooning material are dried azuki beans.

He will sit for quite a while spooning from the bowl to the jar again but then he decides pouring them will be quicker which means we end up with beans everywhere. Oh well, picking them up strengthens his pincer grip.

**What you need:**

- Two small bowls or a bowl and a jar
- Child sized spoon
- Something to transfer such as dried beans
- A tray

Have everything set up on the tray, first time round, show the child how to spoon the beans from one bowl to another, then let them take over.

When they have finished ask them to put all the beans into one bowl and tidy everything away.

This is such a versatile activity that you can play around with by changing the type of spooning material, different beans, beads, rice... You can also change the bowls, big bowls, small bowls, bowls made of metal or glass and finally the type of spoon. No end of spooning fun!

As your child gets older try giving them several bowls and different beans so they can test the sounds the beans make when spooned into different bowls.

# Preparing A Snack

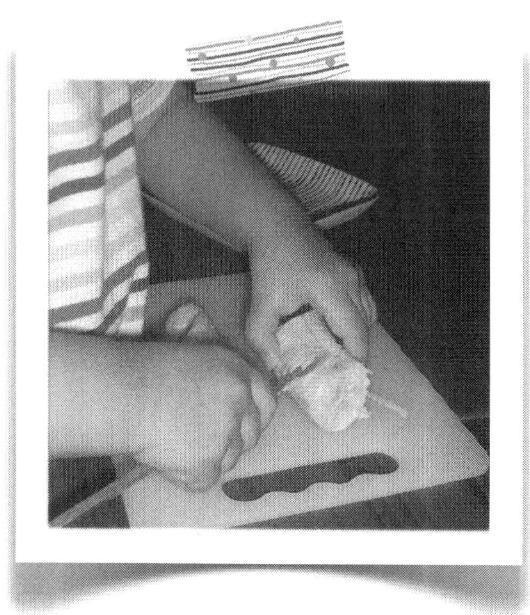

Ebi-kun prepares his own snack in the morning. I get everything out and put it on his shelf then he takes over, he does it in a specific order, it changes slightly depending on what his snack is, today it was a banana

**What you need:**

- A snack station area, this can be as simple as their own shelf or cupboard.
- Cup, plate, chopping board, napkin, knife (one suited to their ability), fork, spoon
- Jug of preferred drink
- Cloth for spills
- Placemat
- Snack items
- Picture instructions (optional)

This is Ebi-kun's routine...

1. Clean up whatever he has been working with before he has his snack.
2. Wash hands.
3. Take out his placemat and put it on the table.
4. Take out his cup and fork, put it on the placemat.
5. Take the milk jug to the table.
6. Put the chopping board, wooden knife, plate, banana and damp cloth on the bench. (We live in a small apartment).
7. Peel banana and put the peel in the bin.
8. Chop the banana and put the pieces on the plate.
9. Wipe hands.
10. Clean up, put the chopping board and knife in the washing up bowl.
11. Take the plate to the table. Sit down and eat the snack, pour milk and drink it.
12. Clean up and put the dirty dishes in the washing up bowl and the placemat back on the shelf.

Ebi-kun started doing this at 18 months old, at first he needed some assistance but by the time he was three he was fully capable of doing it alone and making more complicated snacks. Sometimes I would leave picture instructions on how to make it.

If your situation allows, encourage the child to wash and put away their dirty dishes too.

Some simple snack ideas...

- Cheese and crackers
- Fruit that is easy to chop or peel
- Homemade trail mix
- Dried fruit
- Sandwich
- Veggie sticks (pre-cut) and dip

# Pouring

We have been pouring today. I used 2 small jars and a plastic jug (the glass jug that size is too heavy). I put a couple of drops of food colouring in the water to make it easier to work with and had it all set out on a tray. Keeping a sponge and cloth handy is essential too. Ebi-kun sat for about 30 minutes pouring from one container to another, I had drawn lines on the jar so he could fill to the line but I think it will be a while before he grasps the idea of that, getting the water into the desired container was the challenge.

**What you need:**

- Small jug of coloured water
- A glass or jar
- Cloth for spills
- Tray

Set everything out on the tray then show the child how to pour from the jug into the jar. Playing with water captivates toddlers and learning to pour is a great skill. Be sure to show them how to wipe up spills too, another important skill.

For the best results with this activity you should make sure that the jugs are small enough for the child to manipulate them easily. If the jugs are too big or heavy the child will get frustrated and it will get very messy.

This is an easy exercise to have inside or out, even in the bath. You can make it more difficult by adding lines to the jars for the child to fill to. Once they have got the basics down, try adding a funnel or bottles with narrow necks so that they can hone their skills.

# Threading cards

We made some rainy day threading cards today, having an activity that starts with a craft and then finishes by keeping Ebi-kun busy is a bonus!

**You will need:**

- Scissors
- Hole punch
- Stiff card that will still fit in the hole punch
- Wool/yarn
- Tape
- Pens/crayons

Cut out a shape from the board, it can be anything, I did a butterfly and then a caterpillar with the scrap piece that was left.

Punch holes around the edge of the shape 1~2 cm apart.
Give the card shapes to the child to colour.
While they are completing their work of art, cut lengths of yarn, not too long (I had some scraps and so just used them) add a piece of tape to one end to make a 'needle' this makes it easier for the child to thread.

Once the card has been coloured show your child how to sew using the yarn. I tied the end off so he could sew without pulling the whole thing through. Whilst your child is busy sewing, go and have a nice cup of tea!

Younger children will be happy just ‘sewing’ in and out. Older ones will try to sew around the edge.

For a more difficult project get the child to sew two matching pieces of punched card together.

# Threading Beads

I got these threading beads a while back and he really likes them, if I take them off the shelf he will ask for me to get them out again.

**What you need:**

- A set of threading beads
- Cardboard strips
- Markers to match the colour of your beads

The actual threading exercise is too easy for him now and he soon gets bored so he tried to use the beads in other ways. (Such as swinging them round his head). To try curb this I made pictures of the beads threaded onto cards, increasing with difficulty. He has to copy the picture picking out the right colour and shape of bead.

The set of cards I made wouldn't be any good to you unless you have the same beads which is why I didn't include them as a download, but it is super easy to make your own cards.

Take out your child's beads and set up a pattern, then use some chunky markers and draw the same pattern on a strip of card. If you are a bit of a geek at heart, you can do it on the computer. Start with 4 or 5 cards with just 3 beads then the next set of cards add a few more beads, making the sequences a bit longer and a bit harder each time.

When you come to present the activity, show the child how to first select the beads to match the card and then how to thread them onto the string, finally show to check they are correct by laying their threaded string next to the card.

If you have more than one child, you could get the older child to make the cards for the younger one.

If you have a laminator, it is a good idea to laminate the cards so that they last a bit longer.

# Ribbon Weaving

I showed Ebi-kun a new exercise yesterday. He seemed to like taking the ribbons out more than weaving them in though.

**What you need:**

- Ribbon cut a bit longer than your 'loom'
- Clothes pegs
- Wire type shelf (see picture) or a clean grill from the oven
- Basket for holding the ribbon

First we got out his mat, a basket containing lengths of ribbon and clothes pegs and the 'loom' which is a shelf from the ¥100 shop (dollar store) that I have had for ages, I didn't throw it away when we moved because I thought it might come in handy for something!

Then I showed him how to clip the ribbon to the top of the loom. We started at the top left, as you would if you were writing, to reinforce the left to right, top to bottom action used in the English writing and reading system. *

Then he threaded the ribbons in and out, he didn't fill the whole loom because he REALLY enjoyed pulling the ribbons out when he had finished.

* This is an important point to remember when you are doing activities with your child, if the language you are talking to your child with has a writing system that goes from left to right, such as English, then always set out the activity from left to right. The opposite if your spoken language goes from right to left, such as Hebrew. If you are raising a bilingual child, stick to one language throughout the activity and to the direction of the writing system of that language.

# Transferring Using Pincers

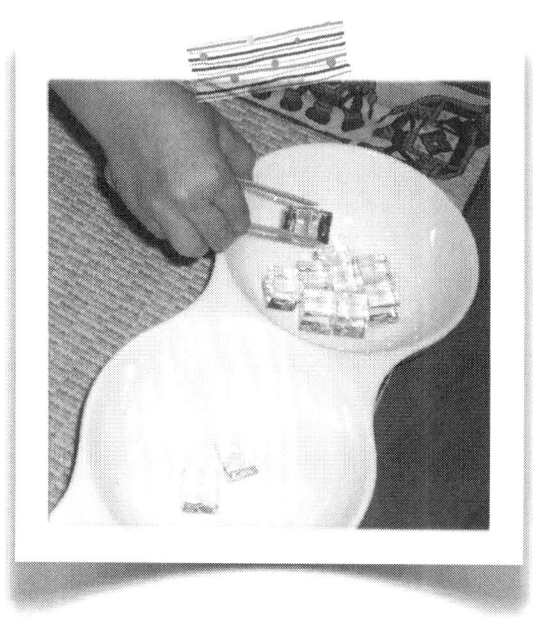

The other day I bought some coloured cubes to add to the ice cooking, I had been looking for those plastic freezer cubes or shapes but couldn't find any and thought these cubes would be just as much fun. They haven't made to the ice cooking session yet but he did enjoy using bamboo pincers to sort the cubes.

**What you need:**

- Tray
- Pincers - we have bamboo ones
- Two small bowls or baskets
- Items to transfer

This exercise is good for strengthening the pincer muscles, the pincer muscles are used for holding a pencil and so children need to work these muscles ready for when they start to draw and write. Any items that are big enough to big picked up with pincers can be used, pom-poms are fairly easy, marbles, not so much. Start with something easy then switch it to make it more difficult.

Show the child how to pick up the items one at a time to move them from one basket to another. Don't be surprised if, when they first do this, they only do a few. It is probably making their fingers ache, like if I asked you to suddenly do 100 press ups.

If their fingers are aching show them a couple of exercises to help with that. First shaking their hands to help get the blood circulating. Then use one hand to squeeze the lower arm and wrist area of the other hand. Finally opening and closing their hands. After doing this for a couple of minutes they should be able to do some more transferring. If you use the computer a lot, you might find these exercises useful for yourself.

# Eye-Spy Bottle

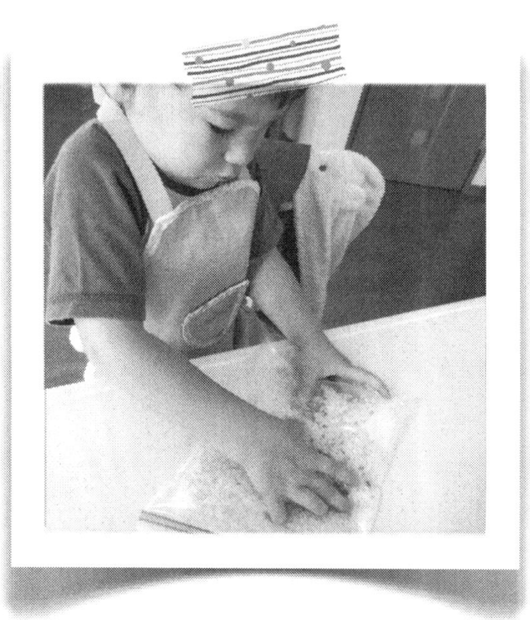

Ebi-kun and I made an eye-spy bottle the other day, I wanted to have something to occupy Ebi-kun in the car as we were planning a long road trip. It was fun to make and could be adapted in so many ways.

**What you need:**

- Empty, clean and dry PET bottle
- Rice, enough to fill the bottle
- Small objects that will fit in the bottle (make this part of the activity, a treasure hunt!)
- Food colouring
- Ziplock bags
- Funnel
- Baking tray (stand the bottle in it when you are pouring to catch stray rice)

First we coloured some rice, yellow and red. To colour it we popped some rice into a ziplock bag, added a few drops of liquid food colour gave it a good shake until the rice was even. Then we hunted around the house looking for objects that would fit in the bottle (we used a 350 ml coke bottle).

I laid the objects out and took a photograph before we put them in the bottle.

We put the objects in the bottle, and poured in the rice using a funnel, Ebi-kun liked doing that part. We didn't fill it right to the top so that there is space for everything to move about. I put on the lid tight. You could glue the top on if you are worried about it getting opened.

Using the photograph I had taken, I printed out the picture of all the objects and laminated it, so it could be used as a point of reference. Challenge your child to find the hair clip, crayon or toy car, etc.

There was some rice left over so he spent quite some time pouring and spooning, he also emptied half the bowl drawer because he 'had' to try the rice in different bowls. I wasn't complaining since I had a stinking headache and any quiet activity was a good activity.

Note: Four years on, that bottle is still in the car and still used on long road trips.

# Marble Muscle Exercise

Yesterday, I introduce a new activity, it is a great pincer muscles activity to strengthen those writing fingers.

**You will need:**

- Polystyrene cube - make dotted shapes using a marker pen
- Golf tees
- Marbles
- Pincers

First we laid everything out on the mat. Then he pushed the golf tees into the cube on the dots that I had drawn. This was quite hard for him at first until he discovered his own technique that worked for him. I had thought about using a hammer but figured we would end up with a smashed up cube!

Once all the tees were pushed in he used the pincers to place the marbles on top of the tees, it's not as easy as it looks!It looked very cool when it had finished. To make it more difficult for an older child you could mark the tees so they had to be pushed in to a certain height.

Specifying what colour marble should go on each tee would also make it more challenging. To put it away, he did everything in reverse order. Pulling the tees out really worked those little muscles.

*This is one of those super exercises, not only was it a bit hit with Ebi-kun but also with his friends.

# Button Cleaning

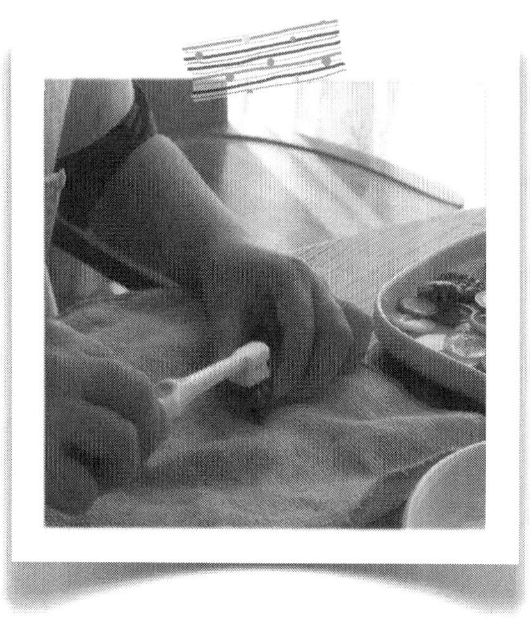

I got a jar of vintage buttons out that a friend gave me for my birthday. They whiff a bit so I came up with a Montessori type of activity for Ebi-kun. (Some might call this child labour but I would call it a button cleaning lesson!)

**What you need:**

- Some dirty buttons
- 3 bowls
- The first had warm soapy water, the second, clean cold water and the third was empty.
- A toothbrush
- 2 towels.

Take a button from the tray, dunk it in the soapy water and scrub with the toothbrush, repeat until happy that the button is clean. Rinse the button in the clean water, dry with the second towel the place in the final bowl.

This kept him busy for getting on an hour, he was totally immersed in his work. Part way through, he discovered that some buttons floated and some sank, so that became part of the process, finding out which ones would float. Once he had cleaned them all we cleared away the water bowls and wiped up then he sat for another hour just playing with the buttons, sorting them and making up stories. Who needs expensive toys? A box of buttons works just fine!

# First Sewing Project

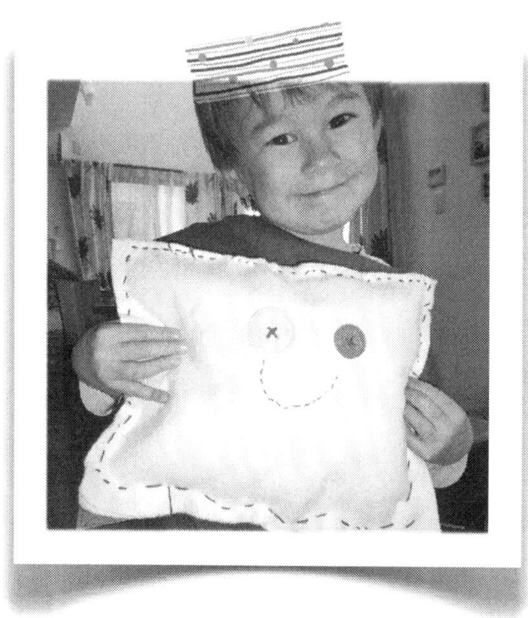

The last couple of days Ebi-kun has been driving me nuts wanting to do his own sewing project. Although he has done some bits of sewing before this is the first time the project was all done by him.

**What you will need:**

- 2 rectangles of felt
- 2 buttons
- Embroidery ring
- A few safety pins
- Stuffing
- Embroidery floss
- Pen
- A large needle*

Start with marking spots for the eyes and a mouth onto the first piece of felt. Put the felt in the embroidery ring. Then show the child how to sew on the buttons, I did the first couple of stitches, modeling how to do it.

I did all the starting and finishing, tying of knots, etc., I wanted the project to be kept simple, so that he would see it through to the end and so he could concentrate on the process of stitching.

Once the eyes are on, stitch the mouth. We used felt buttons but any type with holes will do.

Once the face is finished, place the two pieces of felt together and pin together with safety pins, as an adult I would use normal sewing pins but they stick in you so I reckoned safety pins would be a much better idea.Sew around the edge, leaving a gap for stuffing. As you can see he went over the edge a couple of times instead of up and down, I think it adds to the character! Remove the safety pins.

Stuff with your favourite type of filling, polyfil in this case. Then sew up the hole, I put a couple of safety pins again to keep the stuffing in and the felt flat to make it easier to sew.

*I used a sharp carpet needle and I am sure there are people cringing as I write this BUT like using a knife, I feel that he is less likely to having an accident using a super sharp needle since it glides through the fabric easily, a blunt needle would need more forcing and so making it easier to slip.

# Plant Cleaning

I am not one of those green fingered types and this is the only house plant we have, if you are the same I recommend a Christmas cactus, they are virtually impossible to kill!

**What you need:**

- Water spray bottle
- Cotton wool
- Cotton buds (ear buds)
- Sponge/cloth
- Plant

Have everything set out on a tray, show the child what to do and they let them take over. Spray the leaf with a little water then use the cotton wool and stroke the leaf, start from the centre of the plant to the outside with gentle strokes.

Show the child how to hold the end of the leaf carefully while he works. Use the cotton bud to get to the hard to reach spots. This is a great exercise to talk about plants and either introduce or review parts of the plant.

Be sure to get the child to clean up afterwards. Cleaning up is an important part of the work cycle.

## *Notes and observations*

# Science

***"Education is a natural process carried out by the child and is not acquired by listening to words but by experiences in the environment."***

~Maria Montessori

# Sink Vs Float

We had a busy morning today, I gave Ebi-kun a presentation of the float and sink exercise, I wasn't sure if he would grasp the idea or not but he did quite well. I don't think he can do it unsupervised yet, I will help him again next time and see how it goes, he seem to understand the difference but then forget which bowl was which. He did enjoy doing it though and repeated the exercise 4 times.

**What you need:**

- A tray
- A bowl, half filled with water.
- Two smaller bowls with labels, one with sink and one with float written on it.
- A basket with several objects, some that will sink and some that will float.
- A cloth to wipe up any spills.

To do the work, Ebi-kun half filled a bowl of water, then took an object off the tray and put it in the bowl, if it floated he would then dry it and put it in the 'float' bowl (use labels to help) and if it sank he would put it in the 'sink' bowl.

As the kids get older you can get them to predict before they try. You can also ask the kids to go and find objects around the house to experiment with.

# Taste Testing

Yesterday we did a tasting exercise, this is how we did it...

**What you need:**

- An ice cube tray
- Cards with Sweet, Sour, Bitter, Spicy and Salty written on them
- A selection of foods to sample
- A glass of water
- A bowl for spitting 'horrible' food out (some kids won't need this)
- A cloth for spills
- Camera (optional but worth it)

Set up samples of different food in an ice-cube tray. Make sure you have a good variety and cover each type of food to be tested.

Ebi-kun isn't reading yet so I drew pictures on the label cards to help him remember which was which. I was going to do "salty" too but other than salt itself I didn't have anything suitable to put out to taste!

First I introduced the cards one by one and gave him a small amount of food to represent each one so I knew he understood which was which.

Then he sampled the foods and decided which "taste" they were (this was really funny when he had bitter or spicy, the faces he pulled)! You child might want you to do the experiment too, be prepared to sample somethings you know you don't like.

When he had finished sampling the food we cleaned up and then made a book. He had four pages representing the four tastes he sampled and we looked for foods in magazines that would be suitable for each page to stick on, He wrote his name on a new page for the front cover, punched some holes in the side and tied it all together with a ribbon.

Older children could go into more depth with this or using it as the starting point for a bigger project.

# Magic Milk

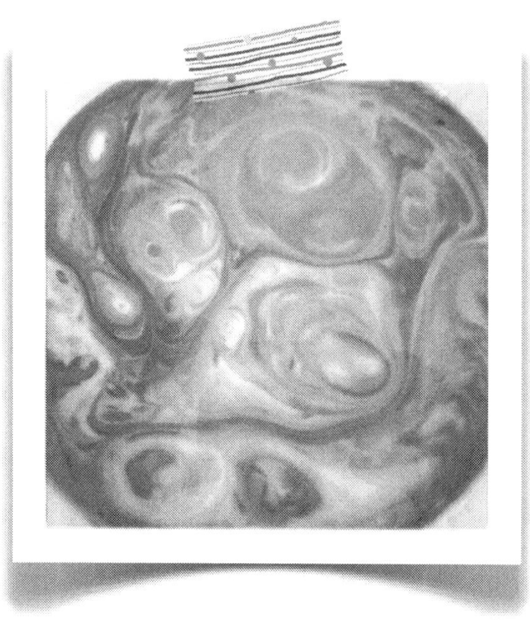

We did this experiment the other day and it got many ooohhs and ahhhhs. Ebi-kun isn't old enough to want to know why and how it works yet, so we will revisit this in a couple of years time. Kitchen science experiments are always fun and the best bit is, you usually have everything you need in the cupboard or fridge.

**You will need:**

- Bowl of full fat milk, (not skimmed or no-fat)
- Liquid food colours, we used red, blue and yellow
- Drop of washing up liquid.

First pour the milk into the bowl and add a few drops of the first food colour, let it settle. Then add the second colour, and finally the third.

Leave it to settle for a minute then add a drop of washing up liquid to the bowl and watch the colours move and swirl by themselves. You need to be quite patient because it is a bit slow to get going but once it does...so beautiful!

If you want to know how this all works, there is a good explanation on this site.
http://www.stevespanglerscience.com/lab/experiments/milk-color-explosion#sthash.j6cK1sPK.dpuf

# Volcanoes

Of course we had to do the volcano experiment, I have been wanting to do this since I took the Montessori course when Ebi-kun was a baby.

**What you need:**

- Clay or plasticine
- A small glass or jar
- Baking soda
- Food colouring
- Vinegar
- Tray

Don't under estimate how much baking soda and vinegar you will need!

We put a small glass in the middle of the tray and then used clay to build the volcano around it. You can use small toys to decorate the volcano if you like. Inside the glass we put a couple of spoons of baking soda and some red food colour. Ebi-kun then poured in the vinegar for the eruption, he loved it and we had to do it again and again and again...

We first did this experiment when Ebi-kun was 2 years old and we have done it every year since, the novelty never wears off! DO make sure you have plenty of baking soda and vinegar, however much you have, I am willing to bet it won't be enough!

If you want to do a more involved volcano lesson, I have volcano 3 part cards available in the shop.
www.my-organized-chaos.com/science/

# Magic Colour Mixing

This is just basic colour mixing really. We have done this a couple of times but used a brush to mix the colours and well, it wasn't very successful. This time I found some pipettes so we could drop the coloured paint into glass jars with water and it worked much better. So much that Ebi-kun declared that it was magic, which of course, it is!

**What you need:**

- 3 glass jars
- Tray to work on
- Jug for pouring water
- Red, blue and yellow watercolor paint, diluted with a little water
- Pipettes for each colour of paint
- Clean up cloth
- Paper to do some painting afterwards.

Ebi-kun set out the three jars and filled them about one-third with water.

Then we practiced using the pipettes for a bit before I bought out the paint. We talked about each colour then I asked him which colour he wanted to add first. "Blue" he said, so he did and then before he added the red I asked him what colour the water would be – he said "blue" so when it turned purple he was amazed. We continued until he had mixed purple, orange and green and then he wanted to do it all again. The third time we did it I drew some squares on a postcard for him to fill in, like a maths equation, and he painted in the boxes – Red + yellow = green. When we talked to my mom on Skype later in the day he could show her what he had been doing and was explaining how the colours mixed together made a new magic colour.

Although this is a very basic idea, to children it is magic so allow them plenty of time to explore.

# Rainbow In A Bag

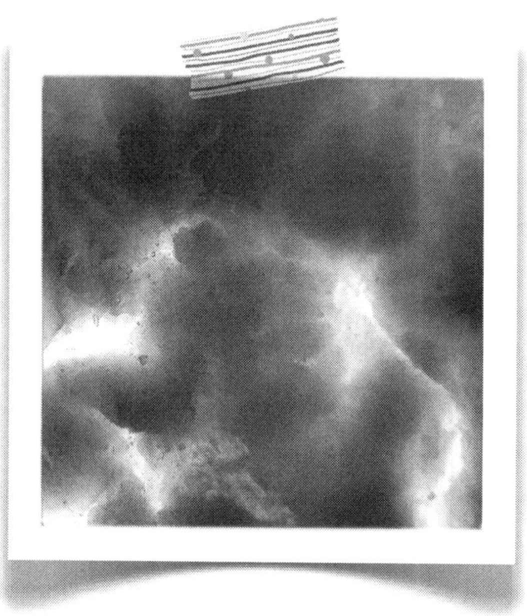

This is another variation on the colour mixing theme. It needs a bit of preparation time but minimal clean up.

**What you need:**

- 1 cup corn starch
- 1/3 cup sugar
- 4 cups water
- Food colour: red, blue and yellow

Put everything but the food colour in a pan and heat and stir until the mixture thickens, remove from the heat and continue stirring for a while.

Separate the mixture into three bowls and add a few drops of food colour one to each bowl, red, blue and yellow.

Mix each bowl well and allow to cool.

Get out 4 ziplock bags, put 2 spoons of mix in the bags as follows

BAG 1 - red and yellow
BAG 2 - red and blue
BAG 3 - yellow and blue
BAG 4 - red, blue and yellow

NOTE - if you think your child can open the bags then tape up the top to prevent a super sticky mess

Making sure it is cool enough to handle, let your little one squidge away. Try to get them to predict what colour they will make, the fourth bag was a leftovers bag but produced a really stunning mixture. If you hold the bag up to a sunny window or put it on a light table, the mixture is semi-translucent and really beautiful, the photograph doesn't really do it justice.

# Primary Colour Canvases

Some artists believe that children should be introduced to art by one colour at a time, so this is a project that we did over the span of a couple of weeks, and the first long project Ebi-kun has worked one.

**What you need:**

Gather a load of bits and bobs, such as shells, lolly sticks, bottle tops, buttons, rice, pasta, pom-poms, any small bits of junk really.

- Acrylic paint, (red, blue and yellow)
- Paintbrush
- 3 cheap canvasses
- White glue and something to spread it
- Varnish

Work on one canvas at a time. We did one a week and tied it in with other primary colour work. FIrst cover the canvas with glue, then stick bits and bobs to it and allow to dry overnight. When the glue is completely dry, cover the canvas with red paint. You may need to touch up any missed spots.
Repeat for blue and then yellow.

If you intend to keep the canvases and they have any kind of food on them then I recommend coating them with varnish to seal them before you hang them on the wall.

## *Notes and observations*

# Science

*"The environment must be rich in motives which lend interest to activity and invite the child to conduct his own experiences."*

~Maria Montessori

# Ice digging

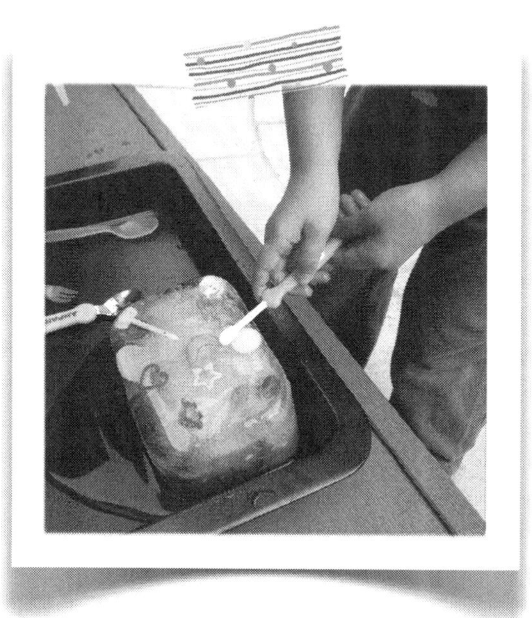

I seem to have one of these permanently in the freezer. It takes a bit of preparation but it will get you plenty of quiet time so it is worth it.

**What you need:**

- Plastic container, like a Tupperware box
- Treasure - anything that you can put in water
- Freezer
- Digging equipment, try using different tools to see what works the best

Take the plastic box and search the house for 'treasure –' ours included plastic animals, beads, buttons and bento picks. I have also used dinosaur bones that were from a kit and coins.

Put a few bits of treasure in the box and fill with water up to about one third of the box. Pop into the freezer. When that layer has frozen add another layer of objects and freeze, then add a final layer and freeze. If you are feeling funky, you can use different coloured water for each layer.

Take it out on a hot day and supply little one with 'tools' to excavate the treasure. This is perfect for outside play but could be done indoors too.

# Ice magic

A quick experiment to try before ice-cooking.

**What you need:**
- Ice cubes
- Bowl of water
- Piece of string
- Salt

Float an ice cube in the water then try to pick it up with a piece of string, it won't work.

Now lay the string on the ice cube and sprinkle on some salt, count to ten and try again - taaadaaaaa

Ebi-kun wanted to try this repeatedly and then eventually just played with the ice and water.

# As Cold As A P.P.P.Penguin?

I asked Ebi-kun what it would be like to be a penguin jumping into the icy water, he said cold. So we did some experimenting.

**What you need:**

- A bowl of icy water
- Plastic glove
- Lard
- Cloth for spills

We set out a bowl of icy water and I asked him to put his hand in it for as long as possible, he managed 4 seconds. He made me do it too.

Then, we put on a plastic glove and covered it with lard, and tried again, this time he kept his hand in for much longer, he described it as being a little bit cold but not too bad, again, I had to give it a go too.

We talked about animals and penguins that live in cold climates and how they use blubber to keep themselves warm. It is a good exercise as a starting point to study the Arctic or Antacrtica.

Or you can use this as part of penguin unit and I have penguin cards in the download pack.

# Ice Cooking

I gave Ebi-kun some bowls, spoons, ladles, you know, general kitchen equipment and a bowl of ice and a bowl of water. He spent a good hour 'cooking' with it. He hasn't shown any interest in spooning for quite a while but he really enjoyed this. He also liked the challenge of walking up and down the steps with a bowl of water trying not to spill any. He enjoyed doing it so much he asked to do it again then next day rather than go down to the park.

**What you need:**

- Kitchen equipment such as bowls of different sizes, ladles, slotted spoons, whisks - whatever you have
- Ice cubes
- An outdoor space

If you want to make it more exciting you can freeze coloured water.

This is one of those really simple ideas that kids will play with repeatedly and perfect for a hot summers day. If it is too hot to do outside, then do it in the bath!

# The Spice Jars

When I am cooking Ebi-kun always want to sniff the spice and herb jars, so yesterday I made up some new work using herbs and spices.

**What you need:**

- A collection of small bottles, covered if they are transparent
- A different herb or spice to go in each bottle that also match the picture cards
- The herb and spices pictures cards from the download file...
- http://bit.ly/MontessoriInspiredFreebies

Put a bit of herb or spice in each of the little bottles. Then put a coloured sticker on the bottom of each bottle and the same colour sticker on the back of the herb or spice card, as a control of error.

For the presentation, I asked him to lay out the plant cards with the names and read what each plant is. Then he took a bottle, sniffed the contents then tried to match it with the picture card. Although I wanted to go through the bottles first, he didn't want to, he wanted to guess from the get-go.

When he had matched all the bottles and cards, he checked his answers by turning the card and the bottle over, to see if the stickers were matching colours.* He got half of them right the first time, so he tried again with the ones he got wrong.

Once he had matched them up, he took the picture cards (no written label) of the dried herbs and spices and tried to match it to the plant, this was quite difficult. The final control of error was to match the dried herb pictures with the labels to the cards that were already down.

* Using a control of error means that the child can check their own work to see if they have got it correct or not.

# Balloon Matching

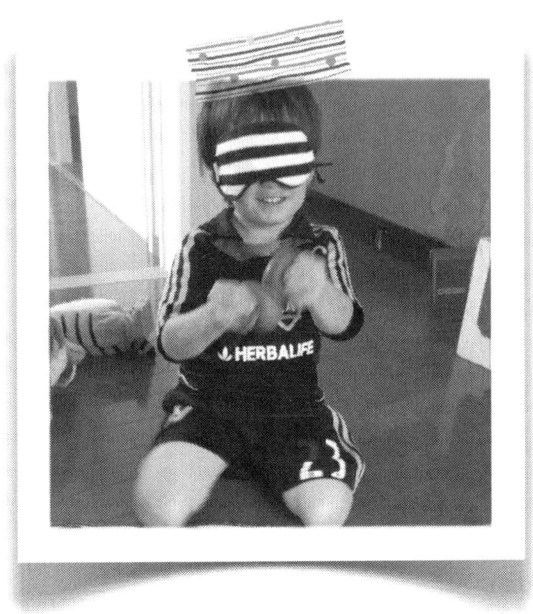


We made these sensory balls the other day, they seem to be as popular with daddy as they are with Ebi-kun.
The sensory balls are easy to make and you can get little one to help you!

**What you need:**

- 4 red balloons
- 4 blue balloons
- Small jug
- Funnel
- Things for filling the balls, we used salt, rice, tiny pasta hoops and flour
- Baking sheet (for easy clean up)

Blow up a red balloon then let it down again, this is to stretch the balloon. Pull the end over the bottom of the funnel. Then pour your first 'filling' in through the funnel, do this over the baking sheet so it will catch any spills.Carefully remove the balloon from the funnel and tie the end, this is a bit tricky and may cause you to use some %$&# type of words!Repeat with the blue balloon with the same filling, so that you have a pair. Draw a small shape on the matching pairs to act as a control of error. Then repeat until you have 3 or 4 sets.

Presenting the work:

- Take out a mat and then the basket with the sensory balls in it and a blindfold.
- Place all the balls on the mat and put on the blindfold.
- Pick up a ball then work through the rest until you find a match, when you have got a match put the pair to one side.
- Continue until all the balls are matched. It is best to model how to do this and then let your child have a go.

Remove the eye mask, you can tell if you make any big mistakes because the balls should be in blue and red pairs. Double check that they are all correct by checking the little shapes you drew on them.

# Lid Matching

I have been wanting to try this for a while and suddenly realised that I had a good collection of jars that we could use.

**What you need:**

- Several jars of different sizes and matching lids
- Rug to work on
- Tray for carrying the jars

First I asked Ebi-kun to roll out one of his mats. Then I showed him the glass jars on the shelf and asked him to take them to the mat, one at a time. The lids were all in a pan we use for pouring exercises. Once he has taken the jars, he took the lids. Then I asked him to put the lids on the jars. Most of them he managed quite quickly, there were a couple he struggled with a bit.

Ebi-kun is going through a stage where he hates wearing a blindfold so instead I asked him to try it a second time, as a big challenge but to do it with his eyes closed. He managed about half before refusing to close his eyes again.

This exercise can be done with boxes that are different shapes or alternatively have a basket with a variety of boxes that open and close with different types of catches or fasteners.

# Marshmallow Sculptures

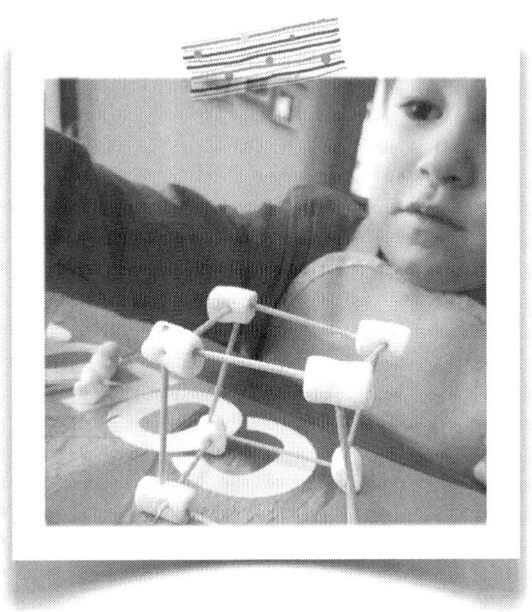

I have been wanting to do this for a while but we always eat the marshmallows before we have chance to try it!

**What you need:**

- Marshmallows - we used the mini ones
- Toothpicks/cocktail sticks

Give them the tools and see what they make.

Ebi-kun made the cube by himself, I just had to assist with some stick holding under his instruction, although I said it was a cube he insisted it was a car! I think when he is older we can try to make more complicated structures maybe even a strand of DNA...

Better to do this activity after lunch rather than just before.

# Musical Glasses

This was a fun musical experiment which of course led onto something else. I got out 7 of our Ikea glasses and put a few drops of food colour in the bottom, mixing some of the colours so that we could make a rainbow.Ebi-kun then poured in the water, I measured the water in the jug so that each glass would have a different amount, an older child could probably do that themselves.

**What you need:**

- 7 similar sized glasses
- Food colouring or watercolour paint
- Jug for pouring the water
- Cloth for spills
- Several things to test when playing the glasses - pencil, spoon, chopsticks...

Pour the water into the glasses. Each glass needs a different amount of water in it.Try out several items to see which makes the better sound. Can you play a tune?

I gave Ebi-kun a spoon and he played sweet music - OK, it wasn't that sweet but he enjoyed it, we then tried using different things to tap the glasses with, the gadget used to get honey out of a pot was the best. I don't have a musical bone in my body but we tried to tap out some tunes then we moved the glasses around and played them again.

When he had had enough of the music playing he asked for a pipette and continued to mix the colours, transferring the coloured water from one glass to another, he sat and did this for ages, together he played with this glasses of water for over an hour and a half, he probably would have stayed there longer if it wasn't dinner time. It was a great activity on so many levels.

# Colour Walk

I didn't have an egg carton because we only get those awful plastic ones, but I did have a fancy chocolate box left over from Valentines. So, we used markers and coloured in each hole. We then went for a wander to see what we could find to put in the various holes. He tried to get a ladybird in the red hole but the ladybird wasn't having any of it and flew off. We have got many allotments around and about so we didn't have to go far and we managed to find something for almost every hole.

**What you need:**

- A card egg box or chocolate box
- Paints or markers

Colour each section of your box. If you use paint, wait for it to dry. Now go on a walk and see what you can find. When you get home make a nature display or a collage with the treasures you have found.

When you have finished keep the box, as the seasons change the items you can collect change too.

# Shake, Rattle and Roll....

We are going to a friend's baby disco party at the weekend so we decided to make some shakers to take with us. This was a bit of a spur of the moment thing which meant I had to look through the recycling to try to find some suitable shaker containers.

**What you need:**

- Empty packaging with lids - good to have a variety
- Pens and stickers
- Dried beans, rice, beads (to put inside)
- Sellotape
- Pumpin' tunes

We got a parmesan cheese pot, a toilet roll middle and couple of boxes. Ebi-kun set to work and put a few spoons of rice, pasta andchopped drinking straws into the various containers then I sealed them with tape. He then decorated with pens and stickers and when he was done I sealed the whole thing by wrapping it in Sellotape. Of course once we were done we had to put some tunes on to test them out. He also sorted them into loud and quiet and picked out which ones he liked best.

This is a great activity to get the wriggles out!

# Card Shopping

The colour tablets are used in a Montessori classroom, which is what we used today but you can use any set of cards that have matching pairs.

**What you need:**

- A set of cards that has two of each image (any of the 3 part cards from the download pack will work)
- Small basket

Lay one set of the cards out on the floor, left to right (if that is the way your language is written) then put the other cards randomly out in the next room. The child looks to see which is the first card then goes and fetches the corresponding card from the other room, puts it in his little basket then when he comes back to the main room he then places the new card under the first card.

If he picks up the wrong card he has to take it back and bring the correct one. It sounds quite simple but for a two year old, they sometimes forget what they have gone in the other room for (happens to us all)!

*The colour cards used here are available from the shop (www.my-organized-chaos.com/store/) or you can use any of the 3 part cards from the download pack.

# Shape Hunt

The other day we needed to go to the drug store which, is only a 10 minute walk away. Before we left I printed out a piece of paper with a collection of shapes on it, we got dressed and took the paper, a pen and the camera with us.

**What you need:**

- Shapes printable from the download file http://bit.ly/MontessoriInspiredFreebies
- Pen/crayon
- Camera (optional)
- Homemade toilet roll binoculars for extra fun (optional)

As we walked along we tried to find at least one of every shape on the list and take a photo of it, we did quite well, we even found an octagon and the only shape which eluded us was the pentagon. The ten minute walk ended up taking an hour and a half!

As a follow up exercise, that I kept for a rainy day, we made a shape book using the pictures we took and any others we could find inside the house. (Ebi-kun really enjoyed it so much we had to do an indoors shape hunt too.)

# Smelling Bottles

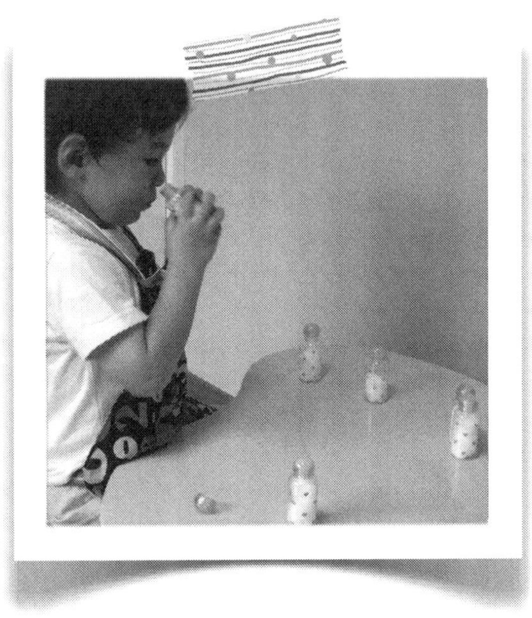

This was quite an easy one to do. I bought 12 bottles, 6 pink, 6 blue but only made up 3 pairs to start with.

**What you need:**

- 6 or 8 small bottles, you need to make them into pairs, so bottles with different coloured caps or lids is a good idea
- Cotton wool
- 3 or 4 essential oils or other naturally scented drops
- 3 or 4 sets of coloured stickers

Put the bottles into pairs. In each bottle I put a cotton wool ball then added a couple of drops of essential oil - real essential oils, not those nasty chemical ones, heaven knows what are in them and I don't really want my child snorting dodgy chemicals. So we have a peppermint pair, lemon pair and a tea-tree pair. (for each pair one is in a pink bottle and the other in a blue bottle)

For a control of error (so the child can check for himself if he is right or not), I put stickers on the bottom of each bottle, green for peppermint, yellow for lemon and blue for tea-tree.

The idea is that the child smells the first pink bottle and then tries to match it to one of the blue ones. Ebi-kun didn't quite get the idea the first couple of times. His reaction to the lemon one was "nice," the peppermint "hmmm" and the tea-tree he screwed up his face, pushed the bottle away and said "Noooooo."

It is quite difficult so I recommend starting with just 3 pairs then adding more. Around the age of three toddler's senses become more sensitive so don't be surprised if they suddenly change their preferences. It is often around this time that they suddenly become picky eaters because of the new sensitivity they are experiencing.

# Mystery Bag

Last night I made a mystery bag, I used to use one when I was teaching so from experience I decided to make the top elasticated which, will hopefully stop the object being pulled out before it has been identified.
Ebi-kun loved the bag, we sat with it for nearly an hour, I had to keep going and finding more mystery objects to go in it.

**What you need:**

- A bag (having an elasticated top helps)
- Several small objects from around the home, pick things with different textures

To play, put one object in the bag without the child seeing. The child puts their hand in the bag and tries to guess what it is. Encourage the child to talk about what they can feel, it is soft, it is fluffy, it is cold, etc.

When they have guessed, the child gets to hide an object in the bag. This is a great game to play with mixed ages/ abilities.

# Sorting Colours

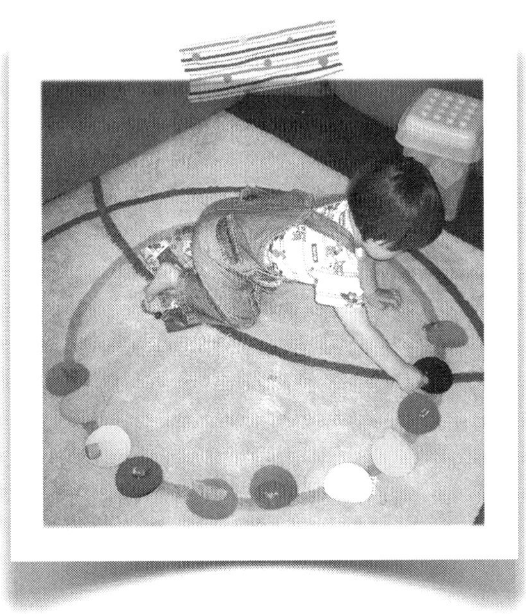

I introduced Ebi-kun to colour sorting this week, he picked it up straight away and has got the activity bag out several times. He has also been sorting other toys into colours, completely unprompted.

**What you need:**

- A set of colour cards from the download file
- http://bit.ly/MontessoriInspiredFreebies
- A bag
- A small item to match each card

In his bag is a set of colour cards and a matching item for each colour. The first time you do this, show the child how to lay the colour cards out. Then take one item at a time from the bag and match it to the card. You can encourage them to say the name of the colour too.

When they have finished, show them how to put everything back in the bag and return the bag to the shelf, the whole cycle should be completed before starting the next activity.

An alternative to this activity is to take a card and find things around the house that match the colour or pick out a colour card and go and hunt for objects the same colour.

## *Notes and observations*

# 123s & ABC’s

*“It is true that we cannot make a genius. We can only give to teach child the chance to fulfill his potential possibilities.”*

~Maria Montessori

# Dinosaur Island

So this morning I knocked up some islands on the computer, as you do!

**What you need:**

- Printable islands from the download file
- http://bit.ly/MontessoriInspiredFreebies
- 55 counters - we used dinosaurs, stating the obvious there!
- Basket to carry your counters in

To play, place the islands all round the room, I made it quite easy to find them the first time then stepped it up a notch the second time round by hiding them up the stairs and in the bathroom too.

The child then takes a basket of 55 objects, we used dinosaurs but shells, pirates, treasure, nuts...anything could be used instead. It is important to have 55 objects so that when the child gets to the last island if he or she doesn't have the correct amount of objects left it means they have made a mistake (control of error) and so they need to go back and check the other islands.

They find an island and then take out the correct number of items out of their basket and put it on the island, if the island has a 6 on it, they need to leave 6 shells, etc.

Perfect for practicing counting and numbers. Often children learn to count to 10 but that is an abstract idea as is the numerals that we use for counting. A child may recognise the numeral 3 because they are three years old but hasn't yet connected the abstract number three to the concrete idea of three objects. Exercises like this one help the child make the connection. Try to add object counting exercises in to your everyday routine, counting socks, slices of banana, wooden blocks. Then introduce the number cards into the mix.

# The Car Parking Game

This is an adaption of the letter recognition game. Ebi-kun can count fine but doesn't 'know' the numerals and since he is really into his little cars, trucks and diggers at the moment I thought it would be a good way to get some practice in. So this is my take on the game.

**What you need:**

- A large piece of card made into a car park with numbers written in the car parking spots
- A set of 10 cards, with spots 1-10 on one side and the numerals 1-10 written on the back
- 10 small vehicles to park

To play, the child takes a spotty card, counts the spots then finds the right parking place, say he picks a card with 3 spots he needs to find number 3 and places the spotty card next to the parking spot (to self check later). He then parks his vehicle in the 3 parking place. Then, continues with the next card until he has used them all up and all the vehicles are parked. Ebi-kun made a mistake and parked the green steam train in 4 instead of 2.

When all the vehicles are parked turn over the spotty cards and check the numbers on the back match the parking place number, if it is correct the vehicle stays put, if it is wrong then the vehicle has to drive out. Once all the cards have been checked the child repeats the exercise with the 'wrong' cards until they are all right.

Ebi-kun enjoyed doing this a lot, I think I need more construction vehicle games!

This is a perfect example of how to adapt a game to the child's current interests, you could set up a similar game with horses and their stable instead of parking lot or little people/ characters going to their houses, pirates and treasure chests...just use your child's imagination.

# Button Math

Ebi-kun suddenly asked me at lunch, "Is two plus two equal four?" He then started counting his fingers, two on the left hand and two on the right to check if he was right, cool. After lunch I had the button tin out (I just bought some super cute buttons) so we ended up doing some impromptu math. We started off just using the buttons but Ebi-kun really needs reinforcement with his actual numerals so I added the number cards into the mix. He did really well and even made some sums up by himself.

**What you need:**

- Buttons (or other counters)
- Number cards from the download file http://bit.ly/MontessoriInspiredFreebies

Make a simple sum such as 2 + 3 =

The child counts out the buttons and places them under each number card. Then adds them all up to find the answer. Then he finds the numeral to match the number of buttons he has as the answer.

This exercise needs to be done with supervision really, as there is no control of error, it was completely impromptu which shows it is handy to have the cards printed to be whipped out at any time.

You can also use whatever the child is into at the time: cars, fairies, crayons, anything that captures their imagination.

# Fallen Leaves

I made a tree and invented a new game for Ebi-kun, really this could be adapted to anything, green bottles on a wall, trains and carriages on a track, sheep in the meadow.

**What you need:**

- A piece of paper with a tree drawn on it (no leaves)
- 10 leaves (we have fabric ones, you could make some from card)
- A basket for the leaves
- Number cards from the download file http://bit.ly/MontessoriInspiredFreebies
- Blu-tac or similar

I stuck the tree to the wall and below it put a basket of leaves and some blutak

Then I stuck a number next to the tree and Ebi-kun had to stick the correct number of leaves to the tree. We talked about how the leaves are falling from the trees now and I told him that he has to check this tree in case the leaves have fallen off.

Then comes the fun part, during the day, whenever I was near the tree, I would pull the leaves off and change the number but I didn't tell him I had done it. Every now and then I hear him shouting 'Oh no, the leaves have fallen off' and he sticks a new set of leaves on. I'm not sure how long this game will last but he is loving it at the moment.

This is perfect for the autumn but I am sure a windy day explanation could be used instead.

Some alternative ideas...

- Washing on a line
- Sheep in a field (they keep jumping the wall)
- Green bottles on a wall
- Baubles on a Christmas tree
- Chicks in a nest
- Candles on a cake
- Flowers in a vase

# The Mini Cafe

Today was lesson day with R-kun. I invited them to the 'Mini Cafe.' They both had a menu with a list of food and drinks and I was the waitress.

**What you need:**

- To set up a table like a cafe, a little vase of flowers, napkins, cutlery and most importantly the menu
- The menu needs to have a long list of snack items such as raisins, banana, cheese, crackers, chocolate, dried apricot, etc., and a selection of drinks. Use whatever you have in at the time.
- Small plates and cups

Ebi-kun ordered raisins and milk and R-kun ordered banana and milk. They had a bit of a shock when their order arrived with just 1 raisin and 1 slice of banana served on a tiny plate and a small sake cup of milk.

When they had finished they had to call the waitress and order again, this gave them plenty of practice and I threw in many questions such as 'Would you like that hot or cold?' 'With or without ice?' I also pretended that I couldn't understand anything Ebi-kun said so that R-kun had to order for him. *

There was much giggling and later Ebi-kun asked if he could have his dinner at the mini-cafe! When the boys are learning about money it would be fun to do this again and charge them for their meals.

*This exercise was for reading and for R-kun, pronunciation, I was teaching him English before his move overseas.

## *Notes and observations*

# Arts And Crafts

***"The child should live in an environment of beauty."***

~Maria Montessori

# Man Hole Cover Art

I can't speak for everywhere in Japan, but in the places I have lived, the city always has cute manhole covers. In Kitakami, where I used to live, they had the onikenbai dancers on the cover. Where I live now is famous for its rose garden and so we have roses on the covers.

**What you need:**

- Large paper
- Wax crayons (chunky ones work best)
- Watercolour paint & brushes
- Some man hole covers

We took out some paper and crayons and did some rubbings on the covers, obviously we picked covers that were on quiet roads or on the pavements.Then when we got home we painted them over the rubbings with watercolours.

Our paper wasn't quite big enough to get the whole of this cover. This exercise is good as it starts with big movement and a walk outside but then the second part is great for quiet time.

# Barrel Rolling Art

Sometimes Ebi-kun will ask to do some painting but I don't want the hassle of getting everything out and cleaning up the mess afterwards. This activity suits both of us, minimal mess but includes paint.

**What you need:**

- A large barrel shaped container, we used an old plastic pretzel jar
- Paper that fits inside the jar/barrel
- Paint
- Random objects for rolling in the barrel, we tried different types of balls, cotton reel, cork, pom-poms.
- Something to dump the paint covered objects in, like a box or dish

We rolled a piece of paper and put it inside the plastic barrel, squirted some paint inside, we used watercolours because that was what we had handy. Then dropped a few objects inside, put the lid on TIGHT and shook and rolled and rolled and shook....

Depending on what you put inside, it has a different effect on the finished painting. Some of them were very Jackson Pollock like when we had finished.

# Brown Bear

I thought we would try an idea out that I have seen bouncing on several blogs. We got out Eric Carle's Brown Bear book and Ebi-kun picked which animal he wanted to make, a brown bear! I sketched it out on a piece of card, I thought it would be easier if he had some kind of frame to work within. We worked together to make the picture, Ebi-kun got bored near the end and let me finish it off, which I was happy to do, I really enjoyed myself!

**What you need:**

- A large piece of thick paper
- Coloured paper
- Pencil
- Glue
- Brown Bear book (optional)

Take the paper and decide which animal you are going to make. Sketch the animal if it is too difficult for your child to do, don't worry if you don't consider yourself an artist, a two year old is hardly going to be a vicious critic!

Tear or cut up the coloured paper, if you child is just learning to use scissors, this is a great way to use up the mountains of bits of paper they will produce, I should know we are buried in little bits of paper at the moment.

Put glue all over your animal shape and stick on the bits of paper.

# Post-it Art

Not really Montessori inspired but I got quite a bit of quiet time out of this so it is worth mentioning. Ebi-kun got his hands on some 'post it' notes, the semitransparent plastic ones and created a work of art on the window.

He experimented with layering to create different shades and colours and throughout the day he would go back to it and do some more or rearrange it. We ended up with it on the window for quite a while, sometimes I would collect all the post it's and put them in a pile then he would start again.

**What you need:**

- A good selection of post it notes
- A section of wall or window

Give the child the post it notes and let them loose, you might want to define where is an acceptable place to stick them.

You could also draw various facial features on the post-its and let the child make up silly faces or matching upper and lower case letters. There are countless variations you could use.

# Bubble Painting

I tried this yesterday after being inspired when playing in the yard with bubbles.

**What you need:**

- A large box with high sides
- Bubble mix or make your own with washing up detergent and a little water
- A bubble blower for each colour
- Watercolour paints
- Paint pots/jars

Pour some bubble mix into the paint pots, then add some paint and stir well (we used the primary colours, red, blue and yellow). Place the paper in the bottom of the box.

Dip the blower into the paint mix and blow bubbles into the box (with a small child this needs close supervision unless you want bubble patterns all over your house) or do it outside.

We have done this several times and found that some paints work better than others, if it doesn't work so well first time round, try a different type of paint. I have also done it with food colouring and that was a success too. The patterns are very delicate in colour no matter which paint we have used.

# Salt Glitter

Not quite as glittery as silver and gold but Ebi-kun had fun making it and I had not so much fun cleaning up all the salt afterwards, you have been warned!

**You will need:**

- A bag of table salt
- Food colouring.
- Little bowls
- Stirring device (we used a plastic fork)
- Thick paper
- Glue

Pour some salt into a small bowl and add one drop of food colouring. Mix well, we found a little fork did the best trick., and then spread out to dry.

Repeat the process with as many colours as you like. We did yellow, blue and red and ermmm... black, which went grey but looked quite cool on the paper.

Ebi-kun then enjoyed trying to mix the colours, he would guess what colour say red and blue would make - get it completely wrong then be surprised when he got purple. As a colour mixing lesson water and paint would be better but it was fun anyway.

Once you have your coloured salts, take some coloured paper and paint or draw a picture using glue, runny paper glue is probably the best but use some heavy weight paper or card otherwise the paper will wrinkle.

Sprinkle the salt onto the paper and leave to try. When the glue is dry, tip the paper up to knock off any excess salt.

Depending on the glue this might not be artwork to keep so take some photos. I found the salt gets knocked off quite easily.

# Working With The Art Cards

I finally remembered to take a picture while he was working with art cards. I have split the pack so that there are only 10 pairs in the folder at the moment.

Ebi-kun knows a few of the artists already, Van Gogh and Klimt, maybe because they are easiest to say. He usually matches the cards then picks up odd cards and studies them, naming various things...ball, boat, flower, etc.

**What you need:**

- A set of art cards from the download file http://bit.ly/MontessoriInspiredFreebies

First ask the child to set out the cards that have just the picture on them.Next ask them to match the pictures cards with the cards with picture and name on it. Finally ask them to match the names with the labelled picture cards. Even non readers can do this, they will probably start by matching the shape of the words, that is OK and is all part of the word recognition process. Later they will try to match the first letters before finally matching the whole word properly.

Once the child is starting to read you can ask them to first lay out the picture cards. Next use the name labels and place the name label under the correct picture. Finally, they use the cards with the name and picture to check their work.

This exercise is used frequently in the Montessori classroom and you can do it using any of the 3-part cards. You can also use actual objects for the child to match.

For the art cards, practice asking leading questions about the images, for example...

- What kind of mood do you think the artist was in when he painted this?
- Why do you think the artist used so much blue in this picture?
- How do you feel when you look at this?
- What are the people doing in this painting?
- Where do you think the ship is setting sail for?

# About The Author

Every time I make something for a child, or I see that spark of deeper understanding, or I hear a fit of giggles brought on because of something I have created, my heart swells that little bit bigger. I love it. I love the facial expression of recognition, the whoops of joy, and the extra special hugs and cuddles. I know that this is what I was born to do.

As a parent, I feel it's the job of all parents to teach and nurture our children, but it's a skill that doesn't come easily to everyone. Unfortunately, we don't get a manual when that baby pops out!

It is my hope that this book will help busy mamas and papas the world over to make the most of their time with precious little ones, and the time is well spent and most of all FUN!

Jo Ebisujima is a Montessori mom, and the owner of Secrets Of A Rock Star Mom and My Organized Chaos. Helping busy parents take control of their home, children and family so that they have more time for the fun stuff is what rocks her world.

Jo has been blogging for years about her life, raising a bilingual child in Japan and Montessori. She started her personal blog, jojoebi designs, over 6 years ago – pop by and say Hello!

Find Jo:
www.my-organized-chaos.com
www.secretsofarockstarmom.com
www.jojoebi-designs.com
www.facebook.com/MyOrganizedChaosJo

Made in the USA
Lexington, KY
02 April 2014